The Pacifier Fairies

By

Mary Fern

A little note for parents

The aim of the book is to encourage children to make their own decision to give away their pacifiers. They might not make that decision on first hearing the story, so please, give them a little time to consider what they will do.
Bluebell leaves a gift when a pacifier has been left under the bed – so remember to be "prepared" and have something ready to exchange for their precious pacifier.

And a final piece of advice. Please don't get too hung up on the issue of pacifiers. Children will give them up, when they are ready, sometimes a little help and encouragement is all that is needed.

Meet the pacifier fairies. Bluebell and all her friends. Can you get some help to find each of them?

The fairies make sure that all the crying babies have a pacifier. Bluebell is bringing one to baby Jasmine.

Here's mindy bringing Josh and John a pacifier
each.

Buttercup is really worried. She has to deliver a pacifier to a little boy called David, and she's just found out there is only one left in the cupboard in the fairy castle. What is she going to do?

Bluebell goes to see the fairy king to see if he knows what to do. She tells him that Buttercup has taken the last pacifier and if there are any more crying babies the fairies won't be able to help.

Bluebell goes to tell the other fairies about the Kings idea. Everyone thinks it is a great plan. Buttercup thinks that if they collect a pacifier it would be nice to leave a little gift for the boy or girl.

That night Mabel sets off to collect some pacifiers for the babies. Tom has left his under the bed. While he is sleeping, Mabel swaps it for a gift from the fairies.

Carol has just left Susan a fairy gift when she
collected her pacifier and now she is heading back
to the fairy castle.

Just after George fell asleep Fern the fairy
arrived carrying a gift. Very quietly, so she didn't
wake George, she left the gift and took the
pacifier back to the fairy castle.

Buttercup left Lauren a lovely gift for her to open
in the morning. A little present to say thank you
for your pacifier.

Saffron put her pacifier under her bed just before
she fell asleep. Mindy has taken it for the babies
and left her a gift.

Bluebell has just left a present for Savannah, it's wrapped up in a lovely blue box with a red bow. Bluebell is hoping that they might have collected in enough pacifiers now to be able to keep the babies happy.

Fern is so happy now she can go back to work. Baby Milo is
unhappy and Fern knows just what he needs. His very own
pacifier.

It's a been a long night for the fairies and they've all gone to bed now. They are so tired after collecting all the pacifiers.

Check out the other Mary Fern Books

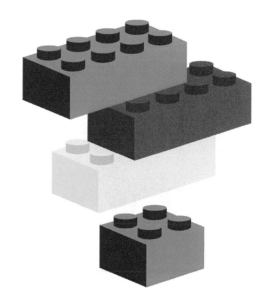

Other books in the Series Cover these topics

Potty Training
Thumb Sucking
Sleeping in your Bed
Going to Sleep

Made in the USA
Coppell, TX
05 November 2023

23844747R00017